Out Of The Shadow
......*a journey to freedom*

Out Of The Shadow
......*a journey to freedom*

ALEXIS STEPHENS

© 2013 Alexis Stephens

All rights reserved. No portion of this book may be reproduced, stored in a retrieval system, or transmitted in any form or by any means – electronic, mechanical, photocopy, recording, scanning or other – except for brief quotations in critical reviews or articles, without the prior written permission of the author. Unless otherwise noted, Scripture quotations are taken from the King James Version.

Published in Orlando, Florida, by SonStar Enterprises

For more information or to contact
Alexis Stephens for Speaking Engagements
visit us at www.AlexisStephens.org

ISBN: 978-1492902263

I want to dedicate this book to those persons who were most instrumental in placing me on this road to discovery of freedom. My Husband-Barry Stephens My Parents-Bishop Woody & Lady Ella Freeman, and my siblings Angela, Ray, Sharon and Teresa. All of you have encouraged me to walk this road and I'm so glad that I did! From the bottom of my heart.....thank you......
I love you!

I also want to say a heartfelt "thank you" to Ross & Tracee you are amazing vision pushers!! I appreciate you and your heart!

It began on a day least expected, there I was going about as usual….without thought….. without fear……without worry. Little did I know that this would be the day that would change my life and take me on a journey that would continue for years.

All of a sudden without warning what started as an innocent action ended in a day filled with pain……a pain that would leave its mark and open up an avenue for the subtle whispers of a bondage masked so well it was invisible, but yet so strong that it took over my identity and left me with a wall that only I could break.

The day was a clear sky beautiful Sunday afternoon, our Worship Service had just ended and I was outside playing around as normal with my friends while waiting for my parents to give the signal that it was time to go. In the meantime, I saw my sister head to her car to run an errand and I knew that she was going to come right back; me being the little sister who always followed her, I jumped in the car to ride along. We weren't gone anymore than 15 minutes before we made it back to the Church. I could see the building from the road, but before we could stop the car, only a few feet away, there was an impact.

Within seconds we had collided with another car. My sister was injured and I knew that I needed to get help for her, but I didn't know that I too was injured until an adult ran over to me and screamed "Oh My God!!! She's Bleeding!!!" Another person quickly ran over to me and put tissue on my forehead and I saw the blood and begin to go into shock. The next thing I knew my Mom & Dad were there and I felt my Daddy put his hand on my forehead and begin to pray.

From that moment on, everything else was a blur until the next day when I looked in the mirror and saw a bandage on my forehead so big that it covered nearly my entire forehead. I was told that when the impact happened, I almost went through the windshield of the car, hitting the windshield so hard with my head that the glass cracked and my forehead split. As a result I had to be stitched up. In the days that followed as my sister and I recovered, I was home from school and she was home from work, I played with my toys as usual and had fun staying home.

The next week I went back to school and my friends greeted me with joy and sympathy. They were glad to see me and I was glad to be back. They were interested in what happened and I must have told the story a hundred times that day, and of course, they wanted to see the damage but all they could see was a huge bandage because the stitches were still there.

Life was now normal again, the worse was over…..so I thought. I was naive to the fact that this would be the beginning of an internal battle that I wasn't prepared to fight.

The day that the stitches came out, after returning home, I looked in the mirror and I saw it……the scar. I didn't think much of it because there wasn't any pain, there wasn't any bleeding; there was just the scar that was still fresh from the accident. That day, I covered it with my bangs and went about the rest of my day.

Upon returning to school after taking the stitches out my routine was the same, with the exception of the fact that now every hairstyle was worn with bangs. I covered the scar as a normal part of my beauty regiment as if it was something that I had done all of my life. But it wasn't, I didn't have a regiment, I had just started combing my own hair……I was only 12 years old.

Beginning with the day that the stitches were taken out, I never wore my hair off of my forehead. This wasn't something that I was told or advised to do, nobody ever told me that the scar was ugly, or that I was ugly, it was just something in me that responded to the scar as shame and my automatic response was to cover it up. I was naive to the fact that the subtlety of shame which had entered into my being as a result of the accident was preceded by fear and the two of them would alter the way that I lived my life.

---- " ----

"Little did I know that this would be the beginning of an internal battle that I wasn't prepared to fight."

---- " ----

You see, I didn't struggle with low self-esteem prior to the accident, I had always heard people say "You are so cute!" I never thought that I was ugly, never heard that word used towards me. Covering up the scar wasn't an issue of low self-worth, but rather it was a response to an experience that happened in my life that I had no control over and my first reaction to it was shame.

The shame that I felt came out of nowhere, but yet it became so familiar to me. It's interesting how an experience beyond our control has an ability to make us feel embarrassed about it. I was ashamed but yet I didn't know why I was ashamed, because I was the victim.

I did nothing to bring this into my life, I didn't solicit this accident, didn't do anything wrong, it happened and I couldn't do anything to make it NOT happen. Why was I ashamed?

Shame is often the first reaction to an experience that leaves you in a vulnerable place, even when you are the victim. It was important for me to realize this because if not, I would still be living with embarrassment. In order for me to move past this I had to:

1. Wrap my mind around the fact that I was the victim of an experience which was beyond my control.

2. Embrace the fact that there was some residue from the experience that I was left with that couldn't be erased.

Because of the shame that I felt having to walk around with this scar, it would have been ideal if I could have just erased it. Not erase the experience, because it wasn't the accident that had me bound, it was the residue from it.

> *"Covering up the scar wasn't an issue of low self-worth, but rather it was a response to an experience that happened in my life that I had no control over and my first reaction to it was shame."*

For me, the residue of the experience was the scar. It was a reminder of what I had been through, a physical reminder. I didn't want anyone to see the residue of the experience. I wanted everyone to look at me the same and continue with life as usual because that's what I did, or so I thought. In reality, every time I looked at the scar I couldn't move past it.

As humans, oftentimes it's hard to adapt to and accept change. But, it's even more strenuous when the change is unexpected. I could deal with the accident and the physical pain, however, I couldn't deal with the impact of the accident because the impact of it shaped my life in a way that was beyond my ability to restrain.

It was very difficult for me to accept the face in the mirror….with the scar. I didn't have breakdowns or meltdowns. I didn't cry when I looked in the mirror, I just altered my look and made it acceptable to my eyes. In essence, I just swept the experience under the rug and kept it moving until I couldn't move anymore because the weight of it had become too heavy.

I don't remember the very day that I realized the heaviness of the experience, but I do remember knowing that I was at a crossroad and either I was going to continue to "BE" what this experience had created of me or I was going to walk out from under it into a place of freedom.

> ***Reflection Moment:***
>
> We never know how much we carry from an experience until the weight of it becomes too heavy. Identify one life experience which had a major negative impact on you.

At what point did you realize the residue was too much to deal with?

When did it become apparent to you that you must rid yourself of this weight or you won't be able to move forward in life?

Looking back in hindsight, I wondered how could I as a 12-year old girl feel ashamed or even embarrassed over something that happened TO ME? I wasn't at fault, I did nothing to deserve it, and I was having a normal day.

Where did the shame come from and why did I feel the need to hide the residue of the experience? The impact of one day became a struggle of more than 27 years and I never saw it coming.

What I now know is that the "something" in me that automatically covered the scar was the part of me that felt I would be viewed differently if my experience became visible. Although the people closest to me, and the ones who were in my circle at the time knew about the accident, I didn't want them to see the residue of it. I didn't mind telling the story, but there wasn't going to be any voluntary show & tell.

> *"In essence, I just swept the experience under the rug and kept it moving until I couldn't move anymore because the weight of it had become too heavy."*

I realized later in life that covering the remains of the experience was a result of an inner anxiety of being rejected. What became my "new normal" was really the silent bondage of fear that had entered into my life and held me hostage.

Not once did I give thought to sympathy and to the fact that people who loved me wouldn't judge me, they would continue loving me. Somehow my adolescent mind unexpectedly, put up a wall between the world and my experience. She wanted the world to see and interact with the person they knew prior to the accident, so she hid the residue in an effort to maintain previous relationships without interruption. Maybe for her the securing of those relationships provided a sense of normalcy, although life would never be normal again.

It's interesting how we can go through something in life and have an automatic response to the incident. While the experience may not be the same, the impact of it has a way of causing damage that is often beyond our ability to handle. Thus, we all have different responses.

Some bury the incident so deep within that they forget the details of it, but yet the sting of pain that creeps into their heart ever so often is a reminder of its existence. Some will walk through the incident and spend the rest of their lives attempting to cover the pain of it with external means. Some will act as if they are invincible because of the incident and as a result lose meaningful relationships because they lack sensitivity. Some will feel defeated in every sense of the word, and never feel strong enough to push forward, even with a helping hand.

"I did all that I could to protect the exposure of the residue and I did it well. I had become a pro-protector of my past."

> ### *Reflection Moment:*
>
> When you look back at that negative experience what were some of the incidents that compelled you to cover yourself in an effort of preventing rejection?

Did you also cover any residue left from the experience?

Who were the people in your life at that time that you didn't want to reject you?

Why was the acceptance of those people so important to you?

I can remember it as if it were yesterday, sitting in a different Dr.'s office whom I would only see once in my lifetime, feeling his fingers go across my forehead and watching his eyes probe around the area as if he were an inspector. Within minutes I was playing with the toys in the corner, however, I could hear the conversation between him and my mother. She asked "Is it permanent?" He responded, "It's permanent." In the days that followed it was as if someone had died, the people that we were closest to asked, "Is it permanent?" and I responded "Yes" and my response was met with "Awww...." and a sad face.

———— " ————

"The impact of one day became a struggle of more than 27 years and I never saw it coming."

———— " ————

Oftentimes people don't realize when you're walking through a negative life experience, sympathy is not always the best response. Simply because sympathy is usually a response of loss, death, long-term illness, bad news. At the time I didn't know that a permanent scar was bad news, inside I felt normal because the accident was over and life continued to move forward. But judging from the reaction of those who knew the final outcome I guess not.

Fast forward to High School and beyond, I never lost a step. I was still called "beautiful," attracted handsome guys, had a trendy sense of style, and I didn't lack any confidence. Wearing my hair in a style that included a "bang" became my signature and although I changed my hairstyle quite often, whatever style I wore was always on point. The people who knew me never questioned it and new people who came into my life accepted it. This residue had become a part of me and had grown with me and my life had become centered around it.

If I couldn't do it with my new signature style, I didn't go after it. I did all that I could to protect the exposure of the residue and I did it well. I had become a "pro-protector" of my past. Nothing, or nobody could convince me otherwise. This mentality caused me to reject those whom I trusted in my life that attempted to get me to come out of hiding and not cover the scar anymore.

They would speak to me with love and attempt to convince me that it wasn't necessary for me to ensure that the scar was covered when I went out in public. I rejected them, I rejected their advice and I didn't trust their opinion. I wasn't mad at them and I didn't respond to them with a cynical attitude, I just silently rejected them. That's another layer of fear.....rejection.

Oftentimes when a person feels rejected he/she will in turn become the rejecter and begin to give what they are receiving. I didn't realize this layer, I thought it was just my prerogative not to accept what they were saying. Their encouragement, affirmations of love for me and willingness to hold my hand as I walked this out were met with.....nothing.

My lack of acceptance of what they were saying to me was shown through my response of continuing to do what I felt I "needed" to do which was cover up the scar. They didn't hold the key to my freedom and no matter how much they loved me, they couldn't unlock me.

Everything in me said "this is ok, you don't have to share with the world what you've been through," but the problem wasn't the world, it was me......I was my own problem.

Reflection Moment:

When someone attempts to give to us it's not always easy to trust and accept what they are giving, even when it's love. Since the incident, who were the people that attempted to love you, show care or concern for you but in return you rejected them?

Inside of me there were desires that couldn't be fulfilled because if so the "scar" would be revealed. Limitations were now a reality, in a way that I hadn't recognized before.

Whenever I would go to the beach or to the pool with my friends, I wanted to swim underwater and splash with everyone else, but I knew that I couldn't, because my hair would get wet and the scar would be revealed. Instead, I opted to just look cute in my swimwear and sit on the side of the pool or just walk in the shallow part of the beach with others who didn't swim.

I wanted to ride in the car with my friend whose Dad had allowed her to drive his convertible. But instead, I opted to drive my own car and let others ride with me because I knew that if I rode in the convertible my hair would fly with the wind and the scar would be revealed.

I chose to avoid doing what I enjoyed because of my fear of being exposed. These decisions were not based on something that anyone said to me, but rather they were a result of my own internal conversations. It was those conversations that drove my actions. My past conversed with my present and my present relayed the information to my future.

The past said "Don't let anyone see the scar or they're going to look at you differently." My present said "Why mess up a good thing? Keep the past in the past and continue to adapt to your new normal." My future said "You're looking good with your bangs, don't change it or they will see the ugly part of you."

It's amazing how one experience seems to have an ongoing conversation with you when in reality its voice is only as loud as the volume that you control.

> ### *Reflection Moment:*
>
> How did the residue of your experience stop you from enjoying certain moments of your life?

When you look back, what do you think the response would have been if you would have exposed the residue that was left from the incident?

One day out of the blue, my friend asked, "Why do you always wear a bang?" and I responded by pulling my hair back and showing the scar only to be met with ".....oh." Nothing else said, no other comment. What was probably about 3 seconds of silence felt more like 30 minutes, it was awkward. We moved forward with the conversation as if there hadn't been any interruption.

> *"It's amazing how one experience seems to have an ongoing conversation with you when in reality its voice is only as loud as the volume that you control."*

This became the ongoing response to those who I allowed to see behind the "bang." Their response became my disappointment because there was a part of me that was looking for some sense of validation and possibly a lifeline that would pull me out from under this cover up and assure me that I was still "the same," but it never happened. So I just kept going…..and hiding.

I felt that validation and assurance was what I needed, but it wasn't because I never lost my confidence. My mind was telling me I needed to hear someone say "You're still beautiful with the scar" but when I did hear those words from people who had influence on me and people who loved me, it wasn't enough to set me free. The reason those words weren't enough was because I wasn't locked up, I wasn't being held, I was free….I was just too afraid to come out.

I knew that this scar in the middle of my forehead was not going to disappear and I was determined to keep people (both old and new) from seeing it. I went through life as if I wasn't bothered by it, because the bondage of fear was so obscure that I really believed that it wasn't a big deal.

I couldn't see while walking through the aftermath of the incident how the residue was now doing more damage than the impact itself. On the exterior, I was enjoying life. I was accomplishing, successful, happy, loved….. but I wasn't free and in reality, I wasn't really happy. How can you truly have happiness when you don't have freedom? You never really know the bondage that you do have until you come face to face with the freedom that you don't have.

Reflection Moment:

When you look back at your own negative experience, was it possible for you to embrace freedom from it a long time ago? What steps would you have taken differently to move towards freedom?

Although I remember the experience and I can recall some of the details of it, I don't remember the pain of the impact. I don't remember the pain of the stitches; I don't even remember the recovery process. But what I do remember is that the experience left me with a scar that I didn't want anyone else to see or even know that it existed because I was afraid of what they would think of me if they saw the real me.

Yes, the REAL me.....unmasked, exposed, not hiding, unashamed.....FREE and A SURVIVOR! That was the real me.

"The reason those words weren't enough was because I wasn't locked up, I wasn't being held, I was free.... I was just too afraid to come out."

The confidence that was on display outwardly didn't match the inferiority that I felt within. It was like gasoline and sugar, not a good mix. Fear came in carrying rejection and now they had opened up the door to shame, the funny thing is none of them were given permission to enter. I was so busy hiding the residue from my experience that I didn't realize I had acquired roommates.

About 17 years after the accident I was preparing to Minister and I heard God say "Alexis, has that scar ever stopped you from moving forward?" and I said "No." I received the revelation that I hadn't been hindered by the scar and when I Ministered that night I gave the testimony and I encouraged those who were in attendance to "move forward from past scars" and we Praised and Worshipped and left encouraged.

Reflection Moment:

How many times did you cover the REAL you just to be accepted by people who are flawed themselves?

How many times did you mask your own pain because you knew that if they saw your pain they would know your story?

How many times did you have to change your story in an effort to continue to cover your story?

But the next day……I didn't have the courage to expose the residue. What happened? Did I not receive an impartation? Didn't I feel strong the night before? Why did I run back into the cave?

You see, even though I had received a revelation, that revelation was the seed, it had not yet manifested into a harvest. I was dealing with 17 years of layers from this experience and it wasn't as simple as it appeared to be to let down the wall. It was easy to Praise and speak boldly around others who encouraged you to walk the tightrope but when it was time to walk it I was going alone and the further I walked, the more the cheers became faint.

I wasn't ready to let the world and even my new relationships in on my experience, I wasn't ready for what they would say, I wasn't ready for how they would react…….not today…..not now. So I continued to hide because hiding was easier than facing rejection.

I was confident enough to wear what I liked and style my hair differently every week, but I wasn't strong enough to defy that one incident and not care what others thought when they saw the residue. I wasn't strong enough to wear my hair off of my face without feeling like everyone I encountered was looking at my forehead.

So in essence, the real me was trapped behind the wall of a scar that was left from an experience in my life that I didn't initiate and I couldn't stop from happening. Trapped....... that's how I felt......day after day, week after week, month after month, year after year for over 25 years I was trapped.

"You never really know the bondage that you do have until you come face to face with the freedom that you don't have."

> **Reflection Moment:**
>
> Take a moment and think of all of the other roommates that have taken up residence in your life as a result of the spirit of fear entering first. Which of those roommates still remain?

On the outside I looked normal, but on the inside I was trapped in an inner prison. Although the doors inside of my inner prison were not locked there were those subtle reminders that coming out of that inner prison, exposing the experience, was not as easy as I thought. Was it vanity? Absolutely not. Was I ashamed of the accident? Absolutely not. What was I hiding? Why was I hiding? Where did this fear come from? I lived my life fearlessly.....or so I thought. These were the questions that I couldn't answer until one day....I was asked a question that began to peel the layers off of my inner prison.

———— " ————

"Fear came in carrying rejection and now they had opened up the door to shame, the funny thing is none of them were given permission to enter."

———— ” ————

The morning began as usual, I was washing my face and as I looked in the mirror, I heard the voice of God ask a question. He said to me "Alexis, does that scar stop you from progressing?" I replied, "No." He said "Does it stop you from feeling beautiful?" I replied, "No." He said "Has it stopped you from accomplishing?" I replied, "No." He then said "So why do you allow it to stop you from wearing your hair off of your face?"

It was at that moment of conversation with God that I realized how I had allowed this one experience to push me to a place of FEAR but I couldn't communicate to anyone or myself what I was afraid of. Fear had its grip on me and it was at that moment my journey of coming out of the shadow began and this time there was no turning back.

There were times prior to this point that I had enough courage to reveal the scar. But those moments were short lived because it was revealed during a time when I felt empowered. I was bold enough to talk about it, but I wasn't free enough to live it.

After I finished talking about it, when I returned home I went back into my inner prison because that was a comfortable place for me. This routine had become my normal, but it wasn't me. It was the new normal established from a place of fear and I was paralyzed by it. Everything in me wanted to just BE ME but the residue from this incident had me paralyzed.

It wasn't the accident, I'd gotten over that, my body had recovered from that. What paralyzed me was the residue from the accident. I couldn't move past the residue, I couldn't move past what was left as a mark of that moment in my life. I couldn't move past the thought of how people would view me if they saw the free me.

> *The Journey To Freedom......*

Because the free me was locked inside of that experience, there were other parts of me that were also locked. The free me held creativity in her, the free me held vision in her, the free me held dreams in her, the free me held the lifeline to someone else's freedom. I was behind the bars of a prison that did not have a lock, but fear made me believe that I couldn't come out.

When I look back I realize that I was waiting on someone else to get me out. I wanted to hear someone else say the right words that would unlock these bars. But the reason that it never happened is because the bars were not locked which meant no matter what I was told it would never be the right words, never be enough words because you cannot put a key in a lock that doesn't exist.

People who loved me would say "Girl, that scar is not that big" and I was disappointed that they said "not that big." They would tell me "It's not that bad" and I would be disappointed when I heard "not that bad." I would hear "You can barely see that scar" and I would be disappointed because they said "barely." No matter what I was told it was never enough because the only one who could say the right words to me WAS ME. I held the key to my inner prison and the freedom that I longed for was in a place that only I could reach.

One day during a conversation with someone I was asked "Why don't you ever wear your hair off of your face?" This time, my reply was different, I actually had to think about my answer because now I'm in an unusual place. I am no longer the little girl who is fearful. The me who longed to be free had become stronger than the little girl who was comfortable living behind the shadow. I had stopped feeding the little girl and her voice was now barely a whisper.

I no longer wondered what people would think when they saw the residue of my experience. I stopped caring how they would react when they saw the scar. I was not focused on whether or not they would still see me as beautiful because the little girl was powerless, she was no longer the voice of fear that stopped me from being free.

———— " ————

And the journey continues.....

———— " ————

Please understand, getting to this place wasn't an overnight task. I wanted to be free more than I enjoyed the confines of bondage and I pursued that freedom little by little. In your quest towards freedom don't make an attempt to tackle it at once, if you keep moving forward inch by inch eventually you will get to the finish line.

That same week after the conversation, I went into the salon and told my stylist that I wanted a style with my hair off of my face. She looked at me with the biggest smile and said "Yes Honey! Finally we are going to let go of this bang!!"

Of course, it was a celebration of sorts but as we continued to joke about it and as she styled my hair I could feel her pulling the hair off of my face and my eyes filled with tears.

The moment that I made a decision to open the doors of the inner prison that had kept me in bondage was met with tears. I wasn't sad or happy, the tears were a result of an emotion of release! They were a sign that the first layer had just been lifted!

Over the next few days my new look was met with an array of "You are beautiful!" to "You finally pulled your hair off of your face" to "I love your hair!" Although I kept my hair pulled back for several days, as soon as I washed it the bang was back. I had moved from being bold enough to talk about it to now being bold enough to walk it out, but the walk was just a short one. I only went around the block; I didn't have enough strength to walk any further.

What happened? I thought all I had to do was just pull my hair off of my face and let people see the real me? Why didn't the feeling of needing to go back and hide go away? What made me want to revert back to that comfortable place?

It wasn't anything that anyone said or did that pushed me back behind the inner prison. There were other layers to this bondage that were there so long they had become invisible, all I could see was the top layer but once the top layer was removed the other layers became apparent.

Coming out from under the bondage of an experience does not happen when you make up your mind to tell your story. Because the bondage is within, you cannot walk in true freedom from the residue until you have broken through the layers of the bondage.

Bondage is nothing more than fear of letting go. We become bound to something because we are afraid of letting go of it. The fear of letting go is fueled through various avenues such as peoples opinions, loss, being forced into unfamiliar territory, change and the list goes on. I was bound to wearing my hair in a way that hid what was left of an experience that I had no control over because I was afraid of people's opinions.

I didn't want to be looked at any differently. I wanted to still be seen as the same cute little girl, beautiful young lady, attractive woman that I was always told that I was, and I felt that somehow people's perception of me would be tainted once they saw what I had been through.

Amazingly, I could care less what they thought of my style, what they thought of the many ways I changed my hair, what they thought of the way I walked or the way that I talked. It never really mattered to me if I was accepted or not, but all of a sudden I cared what people would think of my scar?

> *Now.......the next layer, the reaction of people.*

Why do I care what they think about an experience that I survived? The scar is my reminder of something that took place in my life that could have taken my life! If anything, I should always show the scar so that when someone asks what happened I can tell them "I SURVIVED AN EXPERIENCE IN MY LIFE THAT SOME PEOPLE WOULD NOT HAVE BEEN ABLE TO WALK OUT OF!"

Whew!! When the layer of caring about what other people thought of what I had been through was broken, the fear that kept me hidden in my inner prison was broken! The insecurity of how I looked was broken! The fear of not being viewed as the cute little girl, the beautiful young lady, the attractive woman was broken! The prison walls came tumbling down and I walked out of the shadow of that experience.

As long as I allowed the fear of rejection and negative responses from people to live within me, I was bound. But the moment that I killed it by turning this negative experience into a positive perspective I became free. What I realized is that both the experience and the aftermath of it were all a part of my life story and if I allowed others to define the value of my life by the way they responded to the outward scars that are a result of a moment in my story, I am devaluing myself.

Your story may not be pretty, but it's YOUR STORY. Don't allow people to devalue who you are because they judge you according to where you've been. The best teacher of survival is someone who has actually been through something and is now stronger, wiser, increased. People who judge you based on what you've survived are those who have never been forced into an experience where survival was the only way out.

My encouragement to you:

Don't allow the residue of your past experiences to become your daily garments. What you have suffered is a part of your life story; embrace it. You may still feel the sting of it when you think about it but the sting is just a reminder of the pain you've walked through. Allow the words of David to lift you from Psalms 23 when he says "Yea though I walk through the valley of the shadow of death I will fear no evil...."

———— " ————

Today it's a sting; yesterday it was unbearable hurt but you survived it! Embrace you and every place you've endured. Be determined to come out of the shadow of your past and onto a journey of freedom.

———— " ————

Sometimes it is difficult to look at ourselves in the mirror and not be met with condemnation from viewing what we previously missed. This journey should not leave you feeling guilty or humiliated. Don't allow what you now see in yourself to become injurious to you. Don't allow what has been uncovered to become detrimental. Exposure is an opportunity for transformation. Now that you have been given the open door to walk out of the shadow, keep in mind Romans 8:1 that says "There is therefore now no condemnation to them which are in Christ Jesus who walk not after the flesh but after the spirit." SELAH

About The Author

Alexis Stephens is the youngest of 6 children born and raised in Orlando, Florida. She currently serves as Senior Pastor of The Faith Center Church in Orlando, Florida. She holds a Masters degree in Business Administration (MBA). She is married to Barry Stephens and together they are passionate about assisting others in discovering their purpose and focus in life.